# Wild Calm

FINDING MINDFULNESS *in*
# FOREST BATHING

JOAN VORDERBRUGGEN

Castle Point Books
New York

WILD CALM. Copyright © 2019 by St. Martin's Press.
All rights reserved.
Printed in the United States of America. For information, address
St. Martin's Press, 175 Fifth Avenue, New York, NY 10010.

www.stmartins.com
www.castlepointbooks.com

The Castle Point Books trademark is owned
by Castle Point Publishing, LLC.
Castle Point books are published and
distributed by St. Martin's Press.

ISBN 978-1-250-21515-4 (trade paperback)

Design by Katie Jennings Campbell
Composition by Mary Velgos

Images used under license from Shutterstock.com

Our books may be purchased in bulk for promotional, educational,
or business use. Please contact your local bookseller or
the Macmillan Corporate and Premium Sales Department
at 1-800-221-7945, extension 5442, or by email at
MacmillanSpecialMarkets@macmillan.com.

First Edition: June 2019

10 9 8 7 6 5 4 3 2 1

This journal belongs to

The solution to man's probing and puzzlement is really as simple as sitting outdoors and looking at a sunset, feeding squirrels and chickadees, or caring for trees and flowers.

—SIGURD OLSON

# INTRODUCTION

WHAT PLACES COME TO MIND WHEN YOU REALLY NEED TO UNWIND AND RECHARGE? A tropical beach kissed by turquoise waters? A mountain retreat cloaked in the scent of pine? A sunlit spot near a babbling brook or sparkling lake? Or it could be some place as close as a backyard garden or local park, where birds serenade you.

We often look to nature as a place of healing—soothing our feelings of anxiety or stress and rejuvenating our spirit. Maybe we feel comforted by nature because, until just a few generations ago, our ancestors were intimately tied to the natural environment where they lived. Now that more than half of the world's population resides in urban locations, many of us long to reconnect to the scents, sounds (or silence!), and feelings we experience when we're in a pleasant natural location. So it's no surprise that a practice called forest bathing is on the rise. In forest bathing we are invited to spend time in nature, opening our senses and our awareness. It's simple but can be powerful.

## FOREST BATHING AND ITS BENEFITS

Where exactly does forest bathing come from, and how do we know it works? In the 1980s, Japanese researchers found that people who spent several hours of quiet, mindful time in forested natural areas came away with lower blood pressure, lower heart rates, and lower levels of the stress hormone cortisol. The findings were so compelling that the Japanese government designated forests solely for the practice of *Shinrin-yoku* ("bathing in the forest atmosphere"). Immersed fully in nature, people began to experience transformative feelings of enhanced well-being and clarity of thought, lower anxiety levels, and significant improvements in their stress-induced symptoms and diseases.

The experience in Japan is not unique. The physical, emotional, and mental health benefits derived from spending reflective time in nature are backed by decades of research from all over the world.

## GETTING STARTED

While you don't need to be in the wilderness (or even a forest) to gain the holistic health benefits of forest bathing, you will reap the most profound benefits if you have a block of uninterrupted time in the presence of nature. This journal will help you commit to that time and experience.

As a certified forest therapy guide, I've designed these prompts to help you release distracting thoughts and invite you to participate in this therapeutic, rejuvenating, and often inspiring wellness practice of forest bathing. Although this journal can't quite replicate an actual guided forest bathing experience, the easy-to-follow exercises and questions can assist you in deeply and mindfully engaging with the natural world around you, no matter where you live.

What's important is that, just like soaking in a soothing bath, you immerse yourself in the nature connections through the prompts in this book. Release yourself from immediate goals other than to *just be*. No phone. No music. No fitness-related tracking. Leave the dog at home. Give yourself permission to take the time that each nature connection prompt is designed for, to allow you to receive the greatest benefits. Let go of thought as you surrender to the present moment and gifts from the natural world. Soon, feelings of gratitude and peace will start to move in where you once felt stressed and depleted!

Going
to the
WOODS
*is going*
HOME.

–JOHN MUIR

# CHOOSE YOUR BASE

Find a place in nature that you can visit easily and regularly, whether for 10 minutes each day or for a longer time once or twice a week. Look for comfort, quiet, a break from the busyness of people and traffic—a place that allows you to center yourself in the present. You might even consider a few different locations you can alternate visiting, depending on time constraints, the weather, or other factors.

→ Name and describe your base(s) in nature.

# CLEAR *the* CHAOS

What swirling thoughts in your head keep you from enjoying the present moment? Find something in your environment—a stone, pinecone, or handful of grass, for example—that can symbolically hold needless thoughts.

→ Jot down those "needless thoughts" on the stones below. Then cast off your found object with a gesture that helps you to declutter your mind, to be more fully present in nature. (Hint: You can do this before every nature connection.)

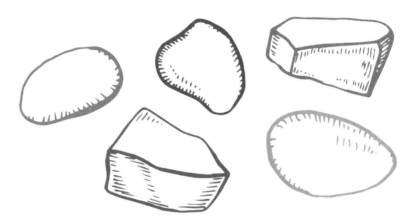

→ Without inviting those unnecessary thoughts back in, capture how it felt to release them.

_____

_____

_____

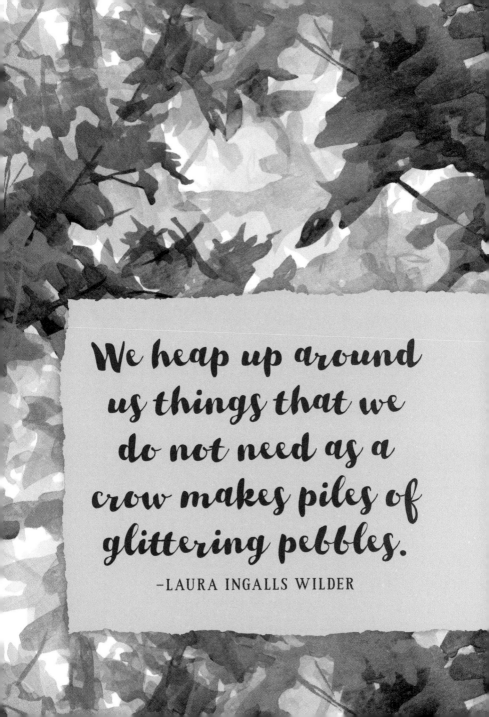

We heap up around us things that we do not need as a crow makes piles of glittering pebbles.

–LAURA INGALLS WILDER

# WILDLANDS

*are off-leash parks for*
*your imagination.*

–KATHY AND CRAIG COPELAND

# FEEL OFF-LEASH

Find a place to sit comfortably where you can observe animals that are "off-leash." This spot could literally be a dog park, but it could also be anywhere you can spend time witnessing an animal's sense of freedom (think: birds, fish). As you watch a particular animal, allow your entire body to feel its movements, as if you *are* this very being.

→ What parts of your body feel activated?

_____

_____

_____

→ After observing the animals for some time, what did you notice about being off-leash? How can you capture this feeling more in your own life?

_____

_____

_____

# CONNECT WITH *a* TREE

Sensing with your body rather than thinking about it, move toward a tree that seems to call to you in some way. Find a place to sit by that tree for at least 20 minutes. Just be present with the tree—touching it, smelling it, gazing at it softly as if it were a dear friend.

➢ Allow yourself to be surrounded by the essence of this tree for as long as you can. What do you feel?

AS I CONTEMPLATE THE TREE I
AM DRAWN INTO A RELATION, AND
THE TREE CEASES TO BE AN IT.

–MARTIN BUBER

# IN NATURE,
*nothing is perfect and*
# EVERYTHING
# IS PERFECT.
*Trees can be contorted,*
*bent in weird ways,*
*and they're still*
*beautiful.*

–ALICE WALKER

# FIND BEAUTY *in* IMPERFECTION

In an image-conscious world, we tend to admire what we deem "perfect" in appearance. But consider how "imperfect" so many trees are. Yet when we look closely at a tree's individual character, each seems more beautiful.

→ Spend time with an element of nature that would not be considered a perfect specimen, noticing its beauty. Draw this, and describe what makes it beautiful to you.

# APPRECIATE UNIQUE PATHS

Find two leaves from the same tree that appear similar in size and color. If they're already on the ground, you can pick them up. If they're on the tree, observe them in place.

→ Record or draw as many subtle differences between these two leaves as you can.

→ What does this teach you about your own view of yourself or others?

In the forest of a
hundred thousand trees,
## NO TWO LEAVES
## ARE ALIKE.
And no two journeys
along the same path
are alike.

–PAULO COELHO

# A WALK IN NATURE WALKS THE SOUL BACK HOME.

## −MARY DAVIS

# GO *with* GRATEFULNESS

Nearly every religion or great spiritual tradition has strong origins or connections to the natural world. Take a slow, gratitude-filled walk in a natural place, allowing yourself to be open to any spiritual feelings that might arise.

→ As you focus on gratitude, capture 10 things that bring joy to your soul in the spaces below.

# TAKE TIME *to* MARVEL

Marvel at the intricate patterned beauty of an acorn, how clouds can look like floating feathers, or how a plant can grow in seemingly impossible conditions.

➤ What marvels do you see around you? Sketch them or write about them below.

➤ How can these realizations translate into other areas of your life?

# NEVER LOSE A HOLY CURIOSITY. STOP EVERY DAY TO UNDERSTAND AND APPRECIATE A LITTLE OF THE MYSTERY THAT SURROUNDS YOU.

—ALBERT EINSTEIN

# Time in nature is not leisure time.

-RICHARD LOUV

# PRIORITIZE *your* NEEDS

There is a Zen quote that goes something like, "You should sit in meditation for 20 minutes every day—unless you're too busy; then you should sit for an hour." We may need nature the most when we are stressed or feel we don't have time for it.

↗ Take a nature break on a day when you really feel you can't afford to commit the time. Allow yourself 15 minutes (or more) to take a walk through a park or natural setting. Write how you feel before the walk, then record how you feel after. What happened?

| BEFORE | AFTER |
|---|---|
|  |  |
|  |  |
|  |  |
|  |  |
|  |  |
|  |  |
|  |  |
|  |  |
|  |  |

# REALIZE *your* MIGHT

Sometimes we feel small and helpless in this world, yet observe in nature what one small being can do! Spend time observing insects or contemplating the impressive outcomes or actions coming from something just as tiny.

→ How can a small act that you can do lead to something that encompasses a greater good?

The creation of
a thousand
forests is in
ONE ACORN.

-RALPH WALDO EMERSON

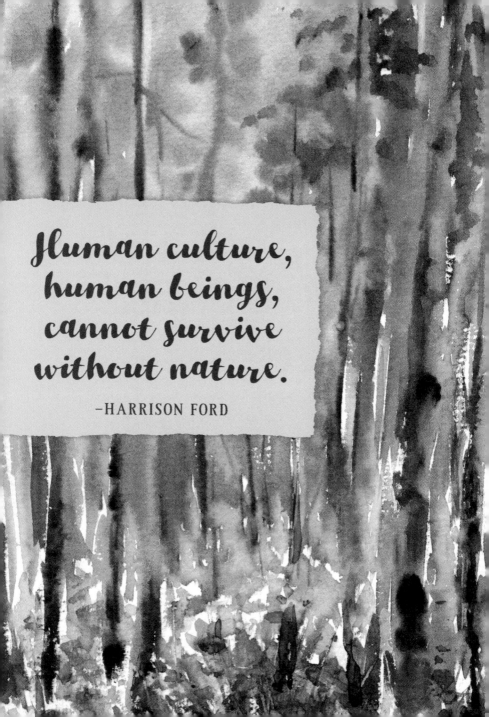

Human culture,
human beings,
cannot survive
without nature.

—HARRISON FORD

# SEE *a* SUPPORT SYSTEM

Write down all the ways that nature supports you and your life. Once you get past the physical basics of air, water, food, and even clothing, go even deeper to explore emotional and spiritual support as well.

→ After you feel you've exhausted your listed items, go for a walk outside and see if nature will reveal a few more!

# UNCOVER *the* POTENTIAL

Take a slow walk in a natural area, paying attention to all the *potential* in nature that lies, mostly unnoticed, around you. What can a small seed or acorn become? Everything in nature eventually changes, but even in the decomposing of a leaf, there is nurturing potential for something else to grow.

→ What are some untapped areas in your life that could lead to growth and transformation?

THERE IS NOTHING IN A
CATERPILLAR THAT TELLS YOU
IT'S GOING TO BE A BUTTERFLY.

–BUCKMINSTER FULLER

Trees
are
POEMS
that
the earth
WRITES
upon the
sky.

–KAHLIL GIBRAN

# LOOK UP *in* WONDER

→ If you can, sit or lie directly under a tree, looking through the canopy and toward the sky. Relax into the earth, allowing yourself time to notice the many subtleties that appear the longer you gaze at and through the tree. Listen as well. When at least 20 minutes of observation have passed, write a short poem or verse that is inspired by what you are noticing.

# STRENGTHEN CONNECTIONS

What if we treated plants and animals more like beloved relatives and friends? Instead of viewing them as being different from us, why not look at how similar we are? Spend time with a favorite nonhuman being, just enjoying its life force.

→ Do you view it any differently when you notice its *aliveness*?

_____

_____

_____

→ What do you enjoy most about the time spent together?

_____

_____

_____

→ How would you introduce it to a friend?

_____

_____

_____

This oak tree and me, we're made of the same stuff.

—CARL SAGAN

One touch of
NATURE
makes the
whole world
KIN.

–WILLIAM SHAKESPEARE

# CELEBRATE NATURAL BONDS

While spending quiet time in nature, contemplate how some element of the natural world in front of you is connected to other elements around you. Don't forget to include yourself in this interconnected web of nature.

→ Write down all the elements that are interconnected, drawing lines between them in ways that show both direct and indirect connections.

→ How does this realization affect you?

# GROUND YOURSELF

Standing on grass, gravel, sand, or stone, take a deep breath that fills your entire chest cavity. Then exhale slowly and repeat two more times. Inhale deeply again, this time visualizing that you are drawing breath from the ground, through your feet and legs, and into your lungs. Exhale slowly, sending your breath back into the earth. Repeat several times.

→ What words capture how you feel? Circle them, and add your own.

Calm      Energized      Focused

One with the world      Balanced

Renewed      Inspired

_____ _____ _____

_____ _____ _____

→ How can you use mindful breathing to channel these feelings anytime, anywhere?

_____

_____

_____

_____

The Earth is not
something outside of us.
BREATHING WITH
MINDFULNESS
and contemplating your
body, you realize that
YOU ARE
THE EARTH.

–THICH NHAT HANH

TREES LOVE TO
TOSS AND SWAY;
THEY MAKE SUCH
HAPPY NOISES.

–EMILY CARR

# DANCE *with* NATURE

On a windy day, find a place where you can be with, observe, and listen to the movement of trees, grasses, or waves. As much as you are comfortable, allow yourself the pleasure of moving your body to a similar rhythm that nature is dancing to, making sounds or singing along as well.

→ What did it feel like to allow yourself to move in the moment—without thought or self-judgment?

_____

_____

_____

_____

_____

→ How did this activity help you connect more with your own true nature?

_____

_____

_____

_____

_____

# ENJOY *a* DETOUR

We walk to get somewhere. We walk for exercise. We walk for many reasons, but usually it is with a goal in mind. Today, take a detour from the usual place you walk, whether inside or outside, so you can experience some aspect of the natural world. It may simply be a walk that lets you view the sky from inside your workplace or encounter a tree in a parking lot!

⇗ Draw a map showing your usual route and the one that gave you a glimpse of nature, making notes about what you saw and how it altered your experience.

# IN EVERY WALK WITH NATURE, ONE RECEIVES FAR MORE THAN HE SEEKS.

–JOHN MUIR

Trees exhale for us so that we can inhale them to stay alive. Can we ever forget that?

–MUNIA KHAN

# BREATHE *in* GRATITUDE

Trees are absolutely necessary for human life, providing oxygen for us and collecting our exhaled carbon dioxide. Find a place by a tree where you can sit, focusing on your breathing. As you inhale, express gratitude for the oxygen you feel entering your lungs and all it gives you energy to do and experience. As you exhale, be grateful to the tree for cleaning the air and for any unnecessary thoughts or feelings it cleanses from you.

→ Record below some of the thoughts of gratitude you felt on the inhales and exhales.

| INHALE | EXHALE |
| --- | --- |
|  |  |
|  |  |
|  |  |
|  |  |

→ What would be the perfect time each day to practice this brief yet cleansing act?

# RELEASE *the* BURDEN

When you need to grieve or release any type of emotional burden, go to nature. What weight are you feeling right now?

�>Open your heart in the presence of a natural element or place. Let yourself cry, if need be. Nature does not judge. Do this as often or as long as you need to, and allow nature to be a therapist. Jot down a few feelings, revelations, or even just words that come to you.

Nature is
A FAITHFUL
HEALER
of the soul.

–BECCA HARTNESS

You only
have to let the
soft animal
of your body
love what
it loves.

–MARY OLIVER

# LET *your* FEELINGS LEAD

In as natural a setting as you can find, go to an area where there are few distractions. Breathing deeply, allow yourself to gently move around until your body (not your mind) feels an attraction toward an object in nature. Allow yourself to just be with and enjoy that piece of nature using all your senses, but without analysis.

→ Sketch or describe the natural object or element, not from a place of familiarity with this object, but from a place of really sensing and discovering it.

# REVEAL INSPIRED SOLUTIONS

Artists, poets, writers, architects, musicians... many have found inspiration in the natural world. In fact, we are all creative beings. Identify an area in your life that requires a creative solution.

_____

_____

_____

_____

_____

Now, take it outdoors. Go for a walk or sit in an area surrounded by natural elements. *Don't think* about the solution. *Just be open* with all your senses in nature for 15 minutes or more.

→ Write down any creative ideas that may have surfaced from this pause in nature, even if they didn't come to you immediately during or after your time outdoors.

_____

_____

_____

_____

_____

UNDER TREES, THE URBAN DWELLER
MIGHT RESTORE HIS TROUBLED
SOUL AND FIND THE BLESSING
OF A CREATIVE PAUSE.

–WALTER GROPIUS

THE TREE GROWS,
FINDING ITS PLACE
IN THE FOREST.
ITS LEAVES GROW AND
SHED WITH THE SEASONS.
FIRES SWEEP THROUGH;
IT IS SCORCHED
BUT SURVIVES.

—M. AMOS CLIFFORD

# THRIVE *with* SCARS

Find a tree or other natural element that shows marks, weathering, or other signs of damage. Spend some time observing it and just taking in its essence without any analysis of why or how those marks came to be.

→ Now think about the damage you have been through in your life. In what ways have you been scorched or scarred?

_____

_____

_____

_____

_____

→ What could this element of nature reveal to you about resilience or overcoming adversity?

_____

_____

_____

_____

_____

# RISE *with* THE MOON

Find a place where you can watch the moon come up, all the way from the horizon to a high point in the sky.

→ At what phase is the moon right now?

→ As you watch, consider: What message or magic might the moon be revealing to you on this night?

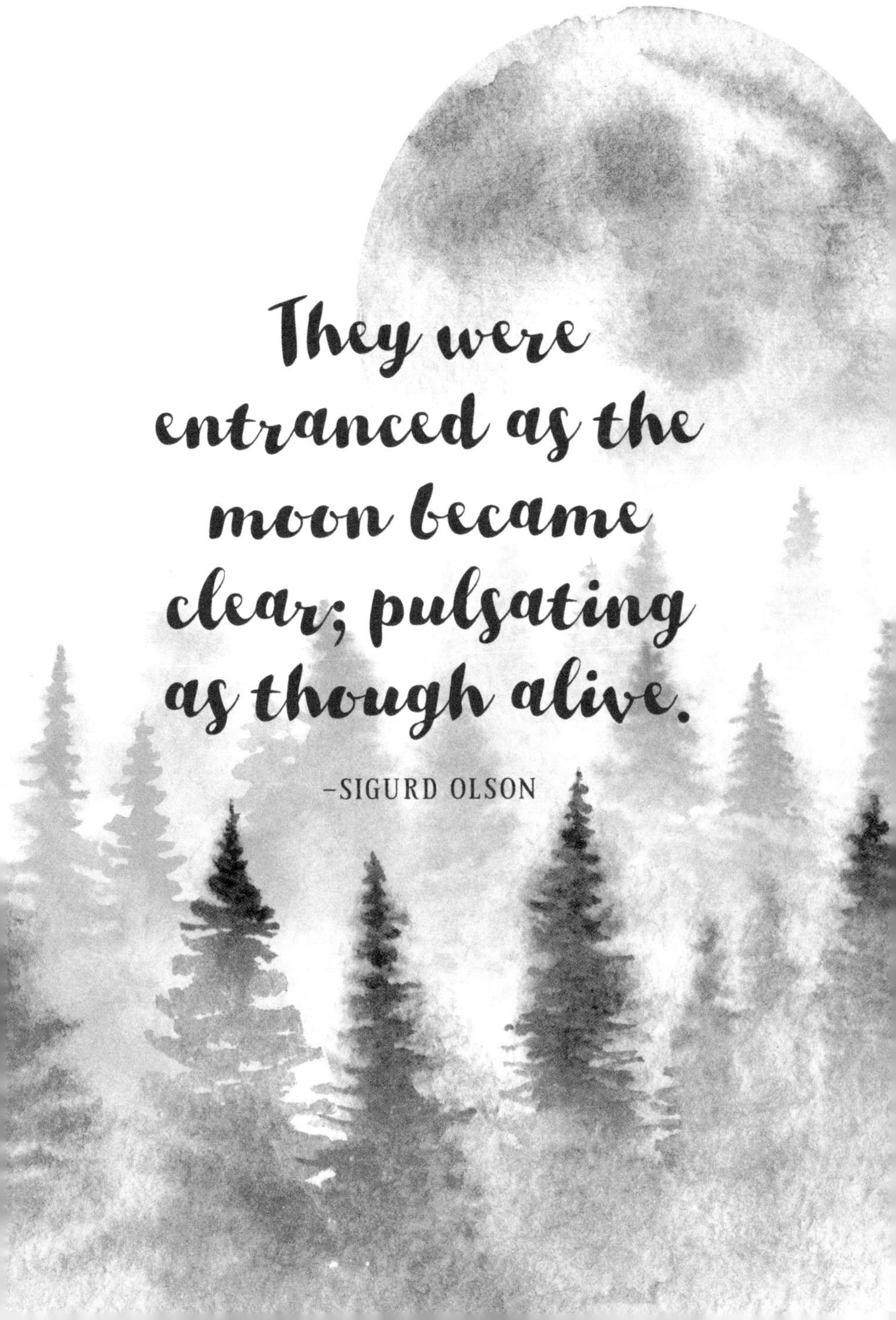

They were
entranced as the
moon became
clear; pulsating
as though alive.

–SIGURD OLSON

NOW I SEE THE SECRET
OF THE MAKING OF
THE BEST PERSONS.
IT IS TO GROW IN THE
OPEN AIR AND TO
EAT AND SLEEP
WITH THE EARTH.

–WALT WHITMAN

# STAY CLOSE *to* NATURE

No matter where you live, you can still find ways to reconnect with the earth on a regular basis. Some ideas: Go camping and sleep on the ground. Open your windows more often. Eat local food that is in season. Wake up with a sunrise, and settle in when the sun sets. Tend to a houseplant. Walk past trees on your way to school or work. The more you can do to align with nature's rhythms, the more benefits you may experience for your mind and body wellness.

→ Keep an ongoing "Nature Connection" list as you adopt habits and rituals into your life to strengthen your relationship with the earth. Jot down notes on what you notice when engaged in these activities.

| NATURE CONNECTION ACTION | NOTES, FEELINGS |
| --- | --- |
|  |  |
|  |  |
|  |  |
|  |  |
|  |  |
|  |  |

# ROAM *in* THE MOMENT

We rarely walk without a goal or destination in mind. It's time to change that! Find a place in a natural setting with boundaries that you know well enough to safely wander and wonder, to explore and discover more deeply.

→ How does it feel to wander without a goal?

\
\
\
\
\
\

→ What do you find?

\
\
\
\
\

# Not all
## those who
# WANDER
## are lost.

−J.R.R. TOLKIEN

IF WE SURRENDERED TO EARTH'S
INTELLIGENCE **WE COULD
RISE UP** ROOTED, LIKE TREES.

–RAINER MARIA RILKE

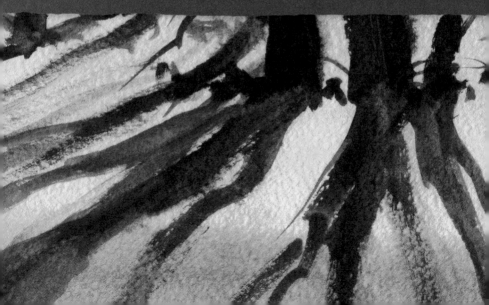

# KNOW WHEN *to* SURRENDER

Spend time with a favorite tree, contemplating how it finds rootedness and strength in its ability to surrender to nature's forces.

→ After just sitting with the tree, consider what in your life you need to surrender or release. Designate below what you intend to let go.

# TALK WITH *a* TREE

Put aside any feelings of self-consciousness and approach a tree as you would a person you'd really like to meet. Respectfully greet it (aloud or quietly) and introduce yourself. Look at it, walk around it, touch its bark and leaves. Rest against it. Tell it about yourself. Ask it questions. And most important, patiently listen for answers.

→ What can you tell the tree that you haven't shared with anyone else?

---

---

→ How does it feel to say what you needed to say?

---

---

---

→ How does it feel to be listened to without judgment?

---

---

---

# TREES ARE SANCTUARIES.

*Whoever knows how to speak to them, whoever knows how to listen to them, can learn the truth.*

–HERMANN HESSE

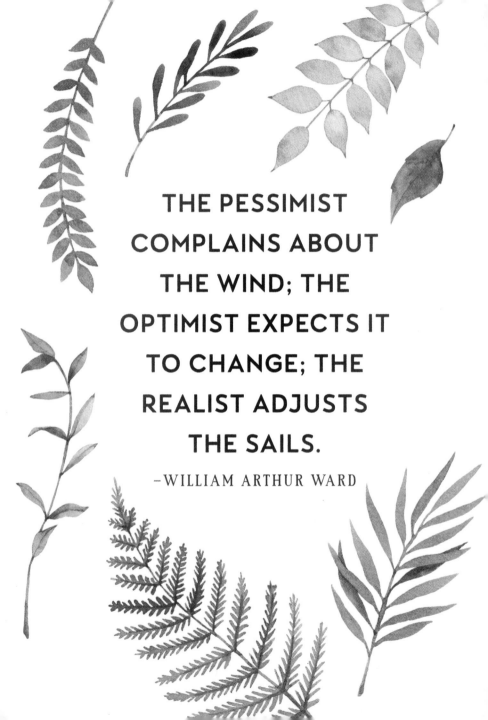

THE PESSIMIST
COMPLAINS ABOUT
THE WIND; THE
OPTIMIST EXPECTS IT
TO CHANGE; THE
REALIST ADJUSTS
THE SAILS.

–WILLIAM ARTHUR WARD

# EMBRACE *the* WIND

On a windy day, allow yourself to fully take in the wind in a safe
outdoor space. Face it and let it flow over you. Focus on how it feels
on your face, your torso, your limbs. Let your feet hold you steady
as you lean into it.

➔ What three words capture the essence of today's wind?

1. _____
2. _____
3. _____

➔ What three words describe how you feel as you meet the wind
head-on?

1. _____
2. _____
3. _____

➔ Are there any lessons the wind teaches you?

_____
_____
_____

# FREE *from* SCREENS

Substitute an hour of screens—TV, video, social media—for an hour of device-free time in nature today.

→ What did an hour of nature give you that screen time would have taken away?

_____

_____

_____

_____

_____

_____

→ How can you do this more often?

_____

_____

_____

_____

_____

UNLIKE TELEVISION,
NATURE DOES NOT
STEAL TIME;
IT AMPLIFIES IT.

—RICHARD LOUV

It is not so much for its beauty that THE FOREST MAKES A CLAIM UPON MEN'S HEARTS, as for that subtle something, that quality of air, that emanation from old trees, that so wonderfully changes and RENEWS A WEARY SPIRIT.

–ROBERT LOUIS STEVENSON

# REFRESH *your* SPIRIT

There is a large and growing body of research on how the aroma (phytoncides) from certain trees and plants helps reduce stress levels and improve health and a sense of well-being, sometimes for a prolonged length of time. Make the journey to a park or forest with plenty of trees, then take time to simply breathe in the forest air.

→ Pay attention to your breath, and to your sense of smell. What do you notice entering your body and soul, and what do you notice drifting away?

INHALE

EXHALE

# FOLLOW *the* SUN

Find a place near you where you have a mostly unobstructed view of a sunrise or sunset, and make an appointment with yourself to really watch the sun's ascent or descent. If you can do this several days in the same week to notice the change in the length of the day or the differences in the sunrise or sunset, all the better.

→ How does this connection with the beginning or end of the day change your outlook on your day? On your life?

_____

_____

_____

→ What metaphors for your life do either the sunrise or the sunset present?

SUNRISE — ● — SUNSET

_____

_____

_____

_____

THERE ARE SO MANY OPPORTUNITIES TO
SEE THE SUN GO DOWN IN THE EVENING
AND THE SUN COME UP IN THE MORNING.

–BURT SHAVITZ

# With the new day comes new strength and new thoughts.

–ELEANOR ROOSEVELT

# GAIN *new* PERSPECTIVE

Many times we think things don't change from day to day. Select something in nature that you can closely observe for several days in a row, noticing that each new day brings with it new change, whether in something as simple as a houseplant's growth or as large as the path of the sun.

→ Record the changes of your natural element in words, sketches, or both.

→ What new realizations come to you when observing the changes in nature over several days?

# GUIDE THE SENSES

Find a place in nature where you and one other person can visit for at least an hour. Take turns gently guiding your partner to pay attention to his or her senses, one at a time, with eyes closed: sound, touch, smell, taste, and finally sight. Allow each of you time to really try to experience what nature can reveal through all the senses.

→ Write down any discoveries you and your partner experience after you both complete the exercise.

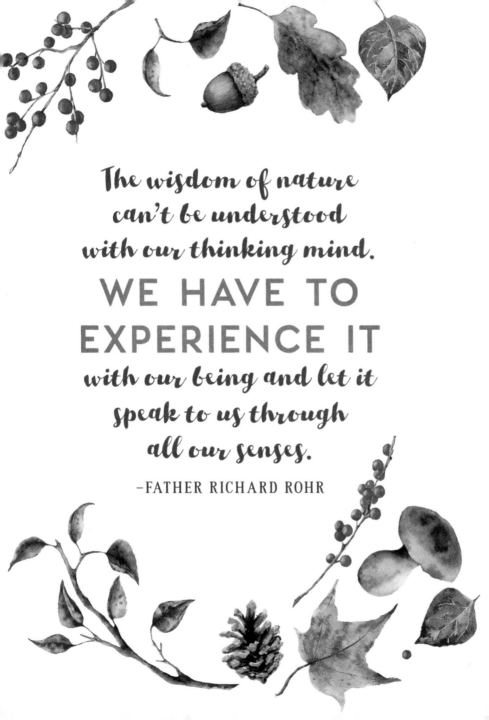

The wisdom of nature can't be understood with our thinking mind.
WE HAVE TO EXPERIENCE IT with our being and let it speak to us through all our senses.

–FATHER RICHARD ROHR

# Storms make trees take deeper roots.

–DOLLY PARTON

# GROW DEEPER ROOTS

Scenes of massive storms on our TV screens and media feeds remind us of the power of nature. Look for and observe trees that have weathered storms in their lives. In particular, focus on their roots.

→ Is there a figurative storm in your life that has helped you grow "deeper roots"?

_____

_____

_____

_____

_____

_____

_____

_____

_____

→ The next time a storm in life comes your way, imagine that you are a tree with deep roots, holding you steady.

# CREATE *on a* NATURAL CANVAS

Spend an hour in a natural area with your inner child. With a sense of curiosity and wonder, find and collect natural objects that have interesting textures, shapes, or colors. Have fun arranging these objects, dropping any fear of perfection or worry that this isn't "good art."

→ Name your piece of art and sketch it below or take a photo, if you'd like, but leave your creation behind to naturally decompose.

→ What does it feel like to engage your inner-child artist?

→ What does it feel like to create a piece of "art" that will naturally fade into the earth?

# ART IS THE CHILD OF NATURE,

*in whom we trace the features of the mother's face.*

–HENRY WADSWORTH LONGFELLOW

I eat my meal
to the singing
of the birds.

–SIGURD OLSON

# REDEFINE EATING OUT

Bring a healthy (and preferably locally raised) meal to an outdoor location, and allow yourself time to slowly savor the flavor and texture of your food. Simultaneously, treat your other senses to the rich sounds, sights, and smells of nature around you.

→ What foods did you enjoy?

→ How did this alter your experience of eating?

# IDENTIFY *a* PORTAL

A portal in nature can be a prompt that helps move you from your cluttered mind to a place where you can begin to become present and focus on your senses. Portals can be physical forms (a creek you cross or a boulder you climb over), or they can be signals (the sound of crunching leaves under your feet or the scent of pine). Find some element in nature that can become a sign for you to move from your thoughts into a more sensory experience in the natural world around you. When you need to, allow yourself to come back through the portal.

→ Draw a representation of your portal.

→ What did you discover on the other side?

BETWEEN
EVERY
TWO PINES
IS A
DOORWAY
TO A NEW
WORLD.

–JOHN MUIR

# I AM IN LOVE WITH THE GREEN EARTH.

–CHARLES LAMB

# EXPRESS *your* FEELINGS

Write a love letter to the earth. Consider including the first time you can remember spending time in nature, how you have grown closer to nature over the years, what you appreciate most, and how you plan to spend even more time together in the future.

# PHOTOGRAPH NATURE'S BEAUTY

Give yourself at least an hour outside (in your own backyard or neighborhood, if possible) to photograph the beautiful things you find in nature. Focus on the tiny or surprising moments of beauty—a pattern of birds sitting on a wire, or a tiny plant emerging from an unexpected place. Don't be surprised if you become completely lost in this activity!

→ Print some of your photos and attach them below. Also frame and display them in your home and at work as reminders to appreciate the simple, unexpected beauty of nature.

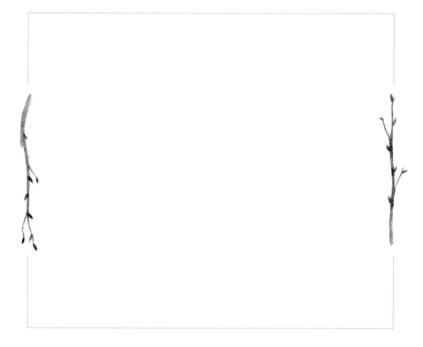

I BELIEVE THE WORLD
IS INCOMPREHENSIBLY
BEAUTIFUL—AN ENDLESS
PROSPECT OF MAGIC
AND WONDER.

—ANSEL ADAMS

Set your course by the
STARS,
not by the lights
of every passing ship.

—OMAR BRADLEY

# BATHE UNDER *the* STARS

Take a night to stargaze. It might mean you need to leave the lights of the city or town, but it's well worth the journey. If possible, lie under the stars and just be there, without distractions.

➜ Sketch the stars in the arrangement they appear to you.

➜ What new perspective(s) does stargazing give you?

# SEEK *out* GREEN

Going outdoors, notice and then record below in some way (through words, photos, or color sketches) all the different greens you see. Really allow yourself to focus on and take in the subtleties in the array of green around you.

→ What does time with all the green vegetation do for you?

_____

_____

_____

→ Make a plan to bring the positive feelings you may have felt into your home by adding more green, whether it be with a live plant or a pillow, or by painting a wall or piece of furniture a shade of green.

# GREEN

*is the prime color of the world, and that from which its loveliness arises.*

–PEDRO CALDERÓN DE LA BARCA

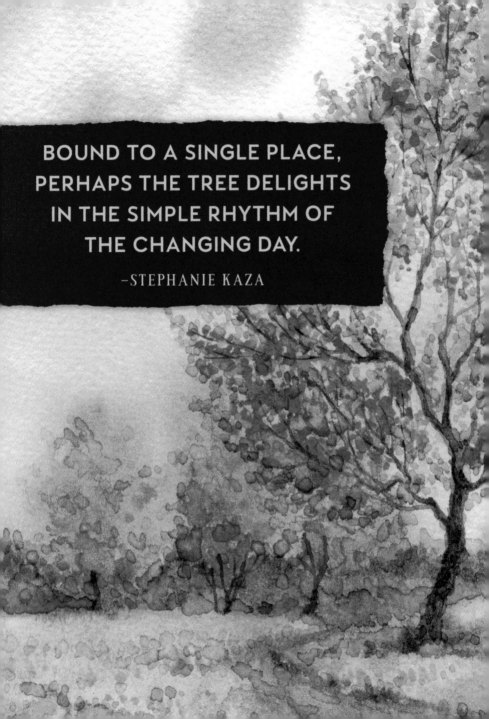

BOUND TO A SINGLE PLACE,
PERHAPS THE TREE DELIGHTS
IN THE SIMPLE RHYTHM OF
THE CHANGING DAY.

–STEPHANIE KAZA

# CONSIDER THE GIFT *of* TIME

Find something in nature that has been in one place for a number of years.

→ After sitting with it for a while and studying the area that surrounds it, write about what it has possibly observed over the course of that time span.

------------------------------------------------------------

------------------------------------------------------------

------------------------------------------------------------

------------------------------------------------------------

------------------------------------------------------------

→ What have you experienced over time that you can share with others just approaching the same place in their lives?

------------------------------------------------------------

------------------------------------------------------------

------------------------------------------------------------

------------------------------------------------------------

------------------------------------------------------------

------------------------------------------------------------

# LISTEN *to a* NEW LANGUAGE

What language of nature are you most familiar with? The sound of the wind in the trees? Waves on a beach? Birdsong? For the next week, pay attention to how nature speaks to you where you live.

→ What makes nature's dialect unique to this particular place?

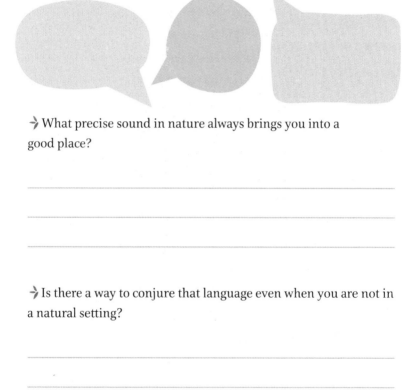

→ What precise sound in nature always brings you into a good place?

→ Is there a way to conjure that language even when you are not in a natural setting?

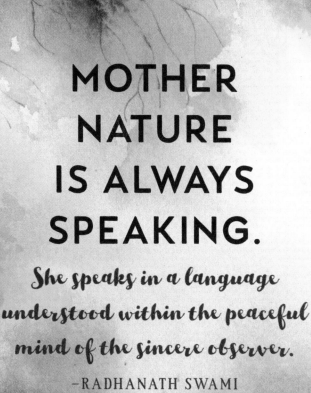

# MOTHER NATURE IS ALWAYS SPEAKING.

*She speaks in a language understood within the peaceful mind of the sincere observer.*

–RADHANATH SWAMI

Nature is not
a place to visit.
It is home.

–GARY SNYDER

# WALK THROUGH *the* YEARS

The natural places we turn to may shift throughout the years due to physical moves or emotional changes. Look back and capture some of the yards, parks, forests, trails, beaches, bodies of water, and more natural elements that have touched your life in a special way.

→ Create a timeline below of those special places.

# SOAK *in* THE SUN

For at least 15 minutes, excuse yourself from something you're doing that you consider unappealing. Take this time to find a private spot of sun, whether you are inside or outside. With eyes closed and a slight smile on your lips, bask in the feeling of the sun on your face and body.

➤ When your time is up, go back to your previous task and notice how you feel about it after your sunshine break. Write down any observations or ways you can allow for more sunshine breaks to brighten your day.

# THE SUN
*does not*
*shine for a few*
# TREES AND
# FLOWERS,
*but for the wide*
# WORLD'S JOY.

–HENRY WARD BEECHER

Knowing trees,
I understand
the meaning
of patience.
Knowing grass,
I can appreciate
persistence.

–HAL BORLAND

# FIND *more* FOCUS

Choose one of these values—patience or persistence—that you feel you need to work on in your life, then find a tree or a patch of grass where you can spend silent time. Consider the question of how the natural element can teach you more about patience or persistence.

→ Listen with your heart. What did you learn?

# GIVE *a* TREE

It is truly an act of selflessness to plant a tree that you may never see fully mature. Find a place that could use at least one tree to enhance the lives of others in the future. It may be a park or a vacant city lot, a place of deforestation, or even your own backyard.

→ Sitting under the shade of a tree you enjoy, make a list of the steps, resources, and people you need to make the planting happen, then do it. Capture the event with a photo!

Date _____

Location _____

SOMEONE'S SITTING IN
THE SHADE TODAY BECAUSE
SOMEONE PLANTED A TREE
A LONG TIME AGO.

–WARREN BUFFETT

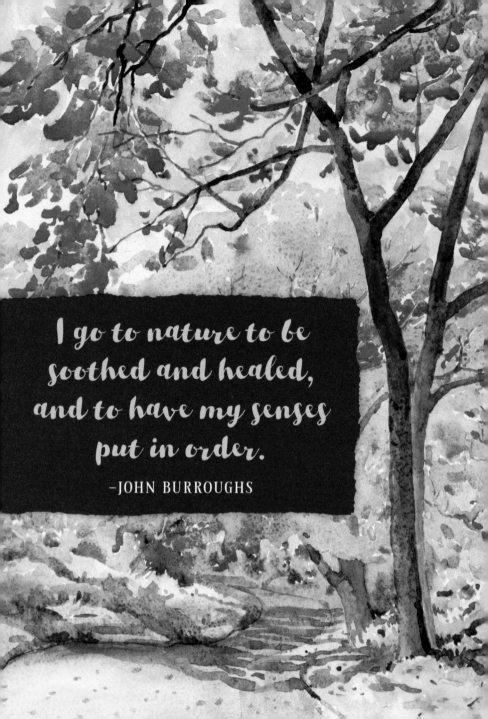

I go to nature to be soothed and healed, and to have my senses put in order.

–JOHN BURROUGHS

# HEAL *with* NATURE

→ Think of someone you know who is stressed or sick, in need of emotional or physical healing. List ideas for natural settings you two could visit to help him or her experience a sense of well-being. If going outdoors isn't possible, can you bring nature into that person's life, touching the senses in some way?

→ Don't forget to surround yourself with nature, if you need healing as well!

# SALUTE *the* SEASONS

Every season has a changing landscape to offer, with new revelations. Consider what the autumn leaves communicate about the beauty of letting go of the past. Instead of wishing winter away this year, what can the bare branches and dormant earth reveal to you? Dressing for the weather, spend quiet, mindful time for as long as is comfortable in a natural setting.

→ What is the most striking thing you see? Sketch it below.

→ Set a date and a place to get out and appreciate the next season as it enters its full glory.

# LET US LEARN
## TO APPRECIATE
there will be times when
the trees will be bare,
# AND LOOK FORWARD
to the time when we
may pick the fruit.

—ANTON CHEKHOV

# MOUNTAINS TALK. CANYONS LISTEN.

—KATHY AND CRAIG COPELAND

# OBSERVE *with* VERSE

Spend quiet, concentrated time simply opening your senses to an element of the natural world.

→ Based on that time and experience, what can you add to the lines of the poem at left?

→ You can add different lines to the poem on different days, depending on new observations.

# APPRECIATE GROWTH

Find the tallest tree you can in a natural area you've chosen to explore. Take time to feel yourself in the presence of this tree and sense its journey to its current size and age.

→ What stories could this tree tell from its long life on this earth?

_____

_____

_____

_____

_____

→ What advice might it have for you about growth?

_____

_____

_____

_____

_____

_____

I FEEL A GREAT REGARD FOR TREES; THEY REPRESENT AGE AND BEAUTY AND THE MIRACLES OF LIFE AND GROWTH.

–LOUISE DICKINSON RICH

The forest
will decide
for each
one of
us what
experience
we need.

–M. AMOS CLIFFORD

# SKIP *the* AGENDA

Find a place where you can spend at least one hour among trees. Just be in their presence, without any agenda or expectations, trying to be as present and mindful as you can as you quietly sit with them.

→ What did the forest decide you needed to experience today?

# SYNC *with* NATURE

Take at least an hour away from a task-oriented schedule and allow your senses to open to any apparent rhythms in nature. You may notice the repetition of waves on a beach, the ebb and flow of wind in the trees, the repeating song of a bird, or even the broader scale of the motion of the sun. Move your body to the rhythm to experience the feeling more deeply.

→ Draw the rhythm as you imagine the sound waves would appear.

→ Where do you feel the sense of rhythm most deeply?

→ What feelings did it unearth?

WHEN ONE FINALLY
ARRIVES AT THE POINT
WHERE SCHEDULES
ARE FORGOTTEN,
AND BECOMES IMMERSED
IN ANCIENT RHYTHMS,
ONE BEGINS TO LIVE.

–SIGURD OLSON

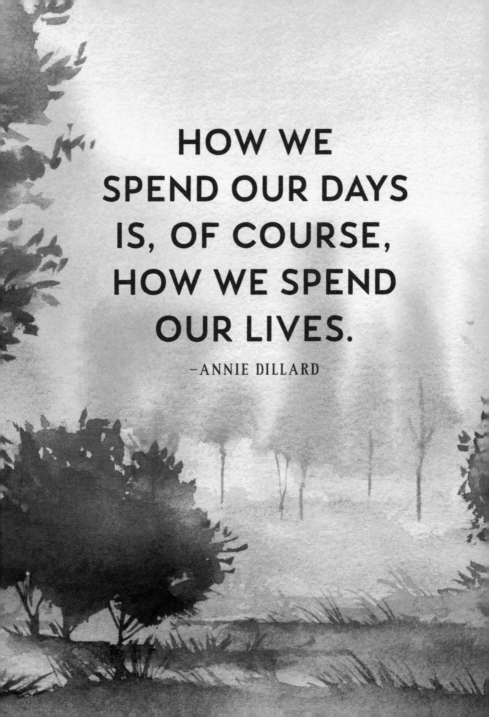

HOW WE
SPEND OUR DAYS
IS, OF COURSE,
HOW WE SPEND
OUR LIVES.

–ANNIE DILLARD

# LOVE *your* LIFE

Yes, time in nature is healing for the soul. But did you know that a day outdoors can significantly boost your body's natural "killer cells" that help it fight disease? Allow yourself an entire day of engagement in a natural area, playing, wandering, and exploring.

→ Write down what your time outdoors taught you about how you want to live each day in the future.

# LEARN *to* PAUSE

In the nest below, identify an aspect of your life that you know will improve with patience, yet are having difficulty in the waiting.

Take your issue to the natural world and sit (patiently!), quietly allowing the slowness of nature's movements (the passing of a spot of light or shadow on the ground, for example) to enter into your very being. This is not easy!

→ How does it feel to slow down, and how might it help you?

Adopt the
pace of Nature:
her secret
is patience.

−RALPH WALDO EMERSON

A LAKE IS A LANDSCAPE'S MOST BEAUTIFUL AND EXPRESSIVE FEATURE. IT IS EARTH'S EYE;

LOOKING INTO WHICH THE BEHOLDER MEASURES THE DEPTH OF HIS OWN NATURE.

—HENRY·DAVID THOREAU

# REFLECT *with* WATER

Water is universally recognized as an element of healing and cleansing. Water is life. Find a clean, natural source of water and spend some uninterrupted time there, no matter its scale, volume, or flow.

→ Sketch the outline of your water feature.

→ Inside the outline, describe your water's features, and what it offers you in insight. Use these prompts to guide you:

**LISTEN.** What do you hear?

**TOUCH.** What do you feel?

**BREATHE.** What do you smell?

**GAZE.** What do you see?

# JOURNEY WITHIN *from* OUTDOORS

Have you ever wondered how to identify your authentic self and what unique gifts you have to share with the world? Allow yourself at least a half day (more if possible) to go on a mini "vision quest" in a favorite natural area.

Pose the above questions about your identity and gifts at the beginning of your journey, then let them go, without judgment or expectation.

→ What do you hear? What is revealed about who you are through this place and your time spent here?

_____

_____

_____

_____

_____

_____

_____

_____

_____

_____

_____

# THE MOST EFFECTIVE PATHS TO SOUL ARE NATURE-BASED.

## –BILL PLOTKIN

People
PROTECT
what they
LOVE.

–JACQUES-YVES COUSTEAU

# GUARD *your* SANCTUARY

After you've spent some days, weeks, or months returning to a special natural area, you will likely notice an even greater appreciation or kinship with your little piece of nature.

→ Write down ways that you can protect this particular area from damage or harm—no matter the size or extent of your actions.

# DEVOTE DAILY TIME

Here and now, on this page, make a commitment to connect with nature each day, no matter how small or brief the connection. Engage all your senses if possible.

→ Here's the plan:

What is the good of your stars and trees, your sunrise and the wind, if they do not enter into our daily lives?

–E. M. FORSTER

# PLACE YOURSELF *in* PEACE

When you can't get to your special nature base where you like to spend time, picture yourself there in your mind with the aid of a photo.

## I AM HERE.

# FIND POWERFUL
# HEALING *in* NATURE

Decades of research ~~~~~~~ he physical, emotional, and mental health benef~~~~~~~~ ~pending reflective time in nature. *Wild C~~~~~~~~ ~* experience the rejuvenating practice of fores~~~~~~~ ~ough:

→ MORE THAN 120 PAGES OF JOURNALING QUESTIONS AND
   CREATIVE EXERCISES TO EASE YOU INTO CON~~~~MPLATIVE TIME

→ EXPERT INSIGHT FROM A CE~~~~~~~~ ~RAPY GUIDE

→ INSPIRATION FROM ~~~~~~~~ ~~ AND WISE QUOTES

No matter where you li~~ ~r how much time you have, this journal will guide you to deeper connections with nature—and greater peace of mind!

JOAN VORDERBRUGGEN came to forest bathing circuitously as an architect specializing in design for healthy environments and through personal healing experiences. After training with the Association of Nature and Forest Therapy, Joan received her certification as a forest therapy guide. She created Bircheart Shinrin-yoku (bircheart.com) in Minnesota's central lakes area, where she lives, introducing others to the therapeutic effects of mindful time in nature. Joan gets outside every day, no matter the weather.

A CASTLE POINT BOOK
for St. Martin's Press
CASTLE POINT BOOKS
175 Fifth Avenue, New York, N.Y. 10010
PRINTED IN THE UNITED STATES OF AMERICA

castlepointbooks.com

US $14.99 / CAN $20.25
ISBN 978-1-250-21515-4

51499 >

9 781250 215154